BUCKET OF AWESOME

The
YOUR-LIFE'S-MORE-
AMAZING-THAN-
YOU-REALIZE
GUIDEBOOK

Kathryn Thompson

FAMILIUS

Published by Familius LLC, www.familius.com

Familius books are available at special discounts for bulk purchases, whether for sales promotions or for family or corporate use. For more information, contact Familius Sales at 559-876-2170 or email orders@familius.com.

Library of Congress Catalog-in-Publication Data
2016958073

Print ISBN 9781944822606
Ebook ISBN 9781944822613
Hardcover ISBN 9781944822620

Printed in the United States of America

Edited by DeAnna Acker
Cover design by David Miles
Book design by Brooke Jorden and David Miles

10 9 8 7 6 5 4 3 2 1
First Edition

To Dan—let's write the rest of our stories together.

CONTENTS

INTRODUCTION

What would you say if I asked you to tell me the story of your life? Would it be humorous? Tragic? Boring? A mind-boggling adventure story I'd have to see to believe? I like to think we all have a healthy mix of those things. There are days when a camera crew following me around would pass out from a boredom-induced snoozefest that would make C-SPAN look like a J. J. Abrams movie. Other days, I am running from place to place, interacting with engaging friends, making life-altering decisions, and saving lives. Yep. I've saved lives, and I bet you have, too.

Did you recognize it?

Do you remember it?

Have you written it down?

Writing your life story is hard. How do you take something as beautiful and complex as an entire human life and boil it down to a few pages? You can't cover everything, and there's no way to be unbiased; you choose which stories to include, and you choose how to tell them.

The first *Drops of Awesome* book was about what we focus on every day as we live our lives. As you worked through that journal, you took time every day to pay attention to, celebrate, and write down all the things you were doing right—your Drops of Awesome. This book is simply an extension of that, digging deeper, going further back. What things have made your entire life Awesome? Let's focus on those. Let's fill an entire Bucket with Awesome.

I'd like to tell you two stories—or, more accurately, one story two ways.

Version A: The summer of 1990, my family rented a beach house with some cousins. My biggest regret about that week is how much time I wasted watching TV. We sat in the beach house watching the same movie over and over again. I can't believe I did that. What a tragic waste! And my siblings and cousins are such jerks. They were old enough to know better but they led me to waste what could have been an awesome week by the ocean.

Version B: One summer, my parents took our family on an amazing vacation to the New Jersey coast. We swam. We played mini golf. We hung out with our cousins. And we watched our favorite movie about a zillion times. To this day, when I hear a line from The Princess Bride, *I think about that summer and what a great time we had.*

There are so many ways to tell a story. I choose version B. Because when I write my life story, I choose to tell a story of joy, a story of triumph, a story of growth, love, and overcoming. I choose to tell a story of Awesome. My Bucket of Awesome.

If you're looking for a book to help you fill a Bucket of Wallowing in Tragedy and Despair, you may need to keep shopping.

Each of our lives are made up of moments, stories, actions, and experiences. Your journey is different from mine. You meet people I will never meet and feel things I will never feel. We both experience joy and pain, though, and we don't always get to choose what happens to us.

We *do* get to choose which stories we tell and how we tell them—even how we tell them to ourselves.

My daughter Ivy professes to hate cleaning her room. It is the worst. There is nothing she likes less. This is what she says. With her mouth. But from her actions, you'd think cleaning her room was her favorite thing ever because she chooses to spend all day doing it.

What should be a twenty-minute chore can stretch on for hours and hours as she puts one thing away and then cries and begs to be released from her My Little Pony–infested prison.

I ask her, "If you hate it so much, why don't you just get it over with and move on?"

"Because . . . waaaahhhh . . . I HATE IT!"

Whenever she wastes an entire day wallowing in needless despair, it makes me think about suffering, about the stories we tell ourselves, and about the reality we choose to live in. It also makes me eat cookies. Because I don't have to share them. Because all the people in my house are either in school, at work, or in a torture chamber of their own making.

She makes choices that lead to her room either staying perpetually clean or becoming a bottomless pit of filth every five to seven days. Those are her choices. She doesn't get to choose the consequences of those actions, things like misplaced toys, Seahawks gear that doesn't get washed before the spirit assembly because it never made it down to the laundry room, or a mom who won't let you do anything fun until you excavate.

So Ivy experiences pain and frustration.

The logical thing to do would be to clean up quickly and then come downstairs for some fun and try harder to keep it clean tomorrow. But six-year-olds are not logical. Neither are most adults.

We make choices, and there are consequences. Sometimes, other people make choices and we get to deal with the consequences of their actions. These can be great, like the consequences you get from working hard at your career or when your college roommate chooses to introduce you to the man who will become your amazing husband. But they can also be awful, like the fallout when you ruin a friendship by gossiping about someone you love or when your car is hit by a driver who chose to get behind the wheel while under the influence of alcohol.

The feelings of joy or pain that we experience are real, and they come without permission. Where our choice comes in is in how long we choose to focus on what happened and how it made us feel (e.g., how long we choose to spend cleaning our room while complaining about how we wish we could stop cleaning it).

Whether you realize it or not, every minute of every day, you are writing and revising your life story. You write as you experience life. You revise as you tell yourself and others stories about your life, how you became who you are, and why you behave the way you do.

You can generate all kinds of Drops of Awesome in

your lifetime, but if you only focus on the negatives, they will become the only things that matter.

The more you tell a specific story, the more ingrained it becomes, the more integral to your final draft. Memories fade over time, and we're left with a pared-down, carefully curated set of stories, mostly created unconsciously—an accidental autobiography.

It doesn't have to be this way. Just as you can choose how to act, you also have power to choose the stories you tell and the way you tell them. You can choose to own your authentic story while deciding how it's written and presented.

As you work along with me in this book, you will be doing two things:

1. You will be choosing how you want to think about your life experience going forward. Will you focus on the joy and the blessings or the pain and the unfairness? You get to decide if your mistakes were dismal failures or learning opportunities. You choose to focus on how you grew from your trials or how they hurt you. This book is an exercise in shifting focus.
2. You will be leaving a legacy to those who come after you, crafting a document you can share to leave a record of your life.

My Grandma Peg passed away a couple of years ago, and I was asked to write and deliver her eulogy. I had known and loved her all my life, but I found I needed to research in order to do her life justice to a crowd of her closest friends and family members.

Writing about how well she cooked beets and grew peas and how sparkly the ceilings were in her living room would not get the job done.

Luckily, she was a personal history goddess, and she left me with ample material to draw from. In the days leading up to her funeral, I immersed myself in words she had written about her life. It was a beautiful life, a life full of service and joy.

It was also a life, I found out as I read, touched with illness, trials, and overcoming heartache.

She didn't wallow. But she did talk about what she did to overcome the hard times. Her autobiography serves as a road map for a good life.

You suffer. You work through it.

You experience joy. You share it.

You mess up. You keep trying.

You feel hurt. You show love.

I always loved her, and she always taught me with her actions to be a good woman, but I have learned even more from her since her death than I did in the thirty years I knew her.

You can do that for those who come after you.

What if you don't have kids? Write anyway.

Your unique life has something worth sharing with the world, whether it's a world of your thirty grandchildren or a neighbor or friend who needs to hear what you have to say. If nothing else, capturing your story will help you decide what to focus on. You will be telling your story to yourself and deciding what to include. This is a powerful exercise that can completely change the way you think about your past.

What if your life story sucks? Write anyway.

There is no life that is a total waste, no story so tragic that some joy can't be found. You are on this earth for a reason. Writing about it just might help you discover it.

It's intimidating to sit down and capture your life in a single volume. You can't write everything, and you can't write it perfectly. So I've broken it down into small, manageable chunks, or Drops of Awesome. Write a Drop today, or even just *start* writing one today. Your record will be one sentence more complete every time you sit down to write. Over time, it will build until you have a document that you and the people who love you or those who come after you will cherish.

It will be inspiring. It will let them get to know the you that matters, the you that got up and kept trying. It will give form to your legacy.

I am not suggesting that you ignore the difficult times in your life; I am suggesting that you don't let those difficult times define you. If you were abused, neglected, bullied, hurt, lied to . . . do not give those who wronged you the power to write your story. Maybe they hijacked it for a second, or possibly for years, but YOU are the one living your life. You are the one writing your story. Take what good you can from your interactions with them, if only that you grew stronger or learned compassion for others who experienced similar abuse, and leave the rest behind.

I have seen journaling exercises that walk you through those experiences, processing them, digging in deep . . . I believe that, with the right guidance, there is value in doing that, but that's not what we're doing here.

The key to making this autobiographical exercise a Bucket of Awesome is focusing on the learning and growth. An experience may not have been the best, but how did it help you become who you are today?

Add dates, names, and places if you have them, but don't let the lack of details delay you from telling your story. Maybe you'll add them in later. Maybe not. What would you give to have a document containing the life story of your mother, your grandfather, your favorite teacher, or your mentor? If it didn't contain dates and details, would it still be valuable to you? Of course it would! Just like one of Da Vinci's preliminary sketches.

Think of yourself as an artist. First create a bare sketch outline, maybe one or two sentences to answer each of these questions. Then fill it in with broad color blocks. Eventually, you may want to add shading and texture, fleshing it out with minute details.

Don't make this more stressful than it needs to be (it doesn't need to be stressful at all). When put on the spot at the pediatrician's office, I sometimes have trouble remembering my own children's birthdates. On-demand information recall is not my superpower, and it's really difficult for me to remember specific details of my life. So, when I am writing my Bucket of Awesome, using an outline to start works well for me.

If you have a hard time getting started, answer the questions that are easy or exciting for you. If one seems too hard, save it for later. This is your story. Tell the parts that speak to you first.

Many of these prompts can be done over and over again, building on them each time. Let's try one as an example.

Think of a time when you forgave.

STEP 1
Sketch It Out: Write basic bullet points about the incident.

STEP 2
Color Block: Talk about what happened. Flesh the bullet points out into sentences. Maybe express how you felt.

STEP 3
Add Texture: Add dates and data, place names and addresses. This may require some research, and it's only a bonus.

As you follow a Drops-of-Awesome approach to not only what you write but *how* you write, the process will feel less overwhelming and more joyful. Think of every sentence you write as a Drop in your Bucket of Awesome.

Set some big goals for this project, and then love all your progress. You can knock this out in ten minutes per day, and after the first ten minutes, you will have something beautiful to show for your work. You can only grow it from there. The more details and examples you add, the richer your story will be.

If the question says, "What is your favorite cookie?", you can respond, "Chocolate chip."

But later, you can add, "My favorite recipe comes from a friend I met in college named Christina Tobler, so my entire family refers to them as the Tobler

Cookies, although I'm the only one who knows how they got this name."

We've provided space in the book for writing, but if you have a lot to say about a particular prompt, feel free to journal it in detail elsewhere.

On that note, if a particular question gets your memories flowing and you find you have a lot to say, don't feel constrained by the questions I've asked or the way they're divided up. If a question about your favorite elementary school teacher reminds you of a powerful lecture you attended in college, write, write, write! You want to capture all those great thoughts as you have them. Sort out the order and structure later.

If writing is hard for you, consider answering the questions verbally and recording your answers. There are inexpensive transcription services online that will type out your answers for you, and you'll be loaded with raw material to polish and print.

This is your project. Tailor it to fit your needs!

You are about to embark on an amazing journey to uncover the best of what makes you who you are. Your journey is unique.

Tell it with patience.

Tell it with love.

Tell it with Awesome.

ABOUT ME

Today's date: _____

Name: _____

Date of birth: _____

Place of birth: _____

Names and birthdates of parents and grandparents:

_____

_____

_____

_____

Names of people in your home as you grew up:

_____

_____

_____

_____

Education:_____

Vocation: _____

Eye color:_____

Hair color: _____

Favorite food: _____

Favorite color: _____

Hobbies: _____

Greatest accomplishment: _____

Thing you're most likely to spend discretionary funds on:_____

Favorite books, magazines, websites, or other reading material: _____

Favorite movies or TV shows: _____

What location do you consider to be "home"?

_____

JUMPSTART

Writing prose is hard. It's overwhelming. Even when I blog or write a book, if I start by telling myself, "Okay; write something brilliant," I'm toast. I have to start small, a few ideas in a notebook, a bullet list in a Word document. The easiest way to begin any writing project is to first dump your brains out on the floor. Everything. What do you know? How do you feel? I'm not talking about chapters or paragraphs or even complete sentences.

For any of these list items that really speak to you, come back later and write a novel about them. But for today, it's lists only.

Starting with a no-one-may-ever-read-this bullet list of ideas is a great way to get your mind powers flowing. We're going to do a few of those now. Over the next several days or weeks, jot down anything you can remember about the following prompts. Bare bones. These will help you remember and give you context for the journaling we'll do later.

Some of these are just a silly walk down memory lane. Others are more serious.

If you're stuck on a specific list for more than a minute or two, don't beat your head against a wall; move on to something you can pound out quickly. Come back to it if you like but not if it's too stressful. It may be helpful to send an email to friends or family and ask if they can help you remember. On the other hand, if you really want to write your own story, you may just want to stick to the things *you* remember. If you've completely forgotten something, that could be a sign that it isn't crucial to your personal story. Or it could be a sign that you're like me and you don't remember much of anything . . .

LISTS

1. What towns or cities have you lived in?

_____

_____

_____

_____

_____

_____

2. What homes have you lived in?

_____

_____

_____

_____

_____

_____

3. List vacations you've gone on.

_____

_____

_____

_____

_____

_____

4. Who have been your best friends through the years?

_____

_____

_____

_____

_____

_____

5. Make a brief list of memories of your . . .

MOTHER:

_____

_____

_____

FATHER:

_____

_____

_____

GRANDPARENTS:

_____

_____

_____

SIBLINGS:

_____

_____

_____

CHILDREN:

_____

_____

_____

6. List your memorable birthday celebrations.

_____

_____

_____

_____

_____

_____

_____

_____

7. What holiday traditions matter most to you?

_____

_____

_____

_____

_____

8. List your teachers or mentors.

_____

_____

_____

_____

_____

9. What were your favorite movies as a child?

_____

_____

_____

_____

_____

10. What are your favorite movies as an adult?

_____

_____

_____

_____

_____

_____

11. List books that have changed you in some way.

_____

_____

_____

_____

_____

_____

_____

_____

12. What are some AHA! moments from your life?

_____

_____

_____

_____

_____

_____

_____

_____

_____

_____

_____

_____

13. What foods do you love?

_____

_____

_____

_____

_____

_____

14. Which songs bring you joy or peace? Excite you
    or pump you up?

_____

_____

_____

_____

_____

15. What are the five places you love the most?

_____

_____

_____

_____

_____

16. What smells send you back in time?

_____

_____

_____

_____

_____

17. What five foods taste like joy to you?

_____

_____

_____

_____

_____

_____

18. Name your three favorite restaurants.

_____

_____

_____

_____

_____

19. List difficult lessons you're glad you learned.

_____

_____

_____

_____

_____

_____

_____

_____

20. What are the three hardest decisions you've ever made?

_____

_____

_____

21. Write a list of values that matter to you.

_____

_____

_____

_____

_____

_____

22. What are a few positive words other people have used to describe you?

_____

_____

_____

_____

_____

23. List the technology you wouldn't want to live without.

_____

_____

_____

_____

_____

_____

24. Which five people have the most influence on you?

_____

_____

_____

_____

_____

_____

25. What small things do you do to make a positive difference in the world?

_____

_____

_____

_____

_____

_____

_____

_____

_____

_____

_____

_____

_____

_____

_____

_____

_____

_____

_____

_____

_____

_____

_____

_____

_____

_____

BiRTH AND BABYHOOD

Now that you've had some practice writing about yourself, let's get into some more details about who you are and how you came to be the Awesome person you are today.

In this section, and also as you continue to work through this book, answer the questions that speak to you, the ones that help you focus on the good in your life, to love yourself and others, to do and be your best. Many people didn't spring from ideal circumstances. If writing about this or any other topic in the book adds negativity to your life, don't include it in your Bucket of Awesome. If our lives are a product of our decisions and experiences, then our memories are a product of what we decide to focus on.

If your birth situation was less than ideal but you can look at the situation in a positive way, perhaps coming to a place where you understand that your difficult beginning gave you strength, resilience, or the determination to do better for your own children, then by all means, use that as the spark for your epic comeback story.

We might as well start at the beginning. Or better yet, before the beginning . . .

Has anyone ever told you about what your world was like before you were born, the story before your story began? Do you know anything about your mother's pregnancy? Did she plan for you? What did she do to prepare for your birth?

_____

_____

_____

_____

_____

_____

_____

_____

_____

_____

_____

What adjectives describe her pregnancy?

_____

_____

_____

_____

_____

What foods did your mother crave while you were in the womb?

_____

_____

_____

_____

_____

What name did your parents almost give you? What do you know about the name they did *give* you? How did they choose it? What does it mean? If no one has ever told you anything about your birth, that is kind of a story in itself, right? If it's difficult to find this information, don't worry about doing a ton of research here. It could be enough to write what you know about your story.

_____

_____

_____

_____

_____

_____

_____

_____

_____

Where were you born? When?

_____

_____

_____

_____

_____

Who was there?

_____

_____

_____

_____

_____

How big were you at birth? _____

Were there any complications?

_____

_____

_____

_____

_____

_____

What other interesting facts do you know about your birth?

_____

_____

_____

_____

_____

Were you ever told about cute things you said as you were learning to speak? What words did you mispronounce?

_____

_____

_____

_____

_____

What were your baby nicknames, and where did they originate?

_____

_____

_____

What was your first solid food or your favorite thing to munch on as a young child?

_____

_____

_____

_____

_____

_____

Do you have any other information about your childhood firsts? First steps? First words? First evil plots to take over the world?

_____

_____

_____

_____

_____

_____

_____

_____

What funny stories do your family members tell about your baby and toddler years?

_____

_____

_____

_____

_____

_____

_____

Did you have a favorite blanket or toy you couldn't live without? When did you let it go?

_____

_____

_____

_____

_____

_____

What were your favorite songs or stories as a young child?

_____

_____

_____

_____

_____

What is your first memory?

_____

_____

_____

_____

_____

_____

_____

_____

_____

_____

_____

CHILDHOOD

I have a difficult time remembering details about my childhood. Most of my memories come as feelings and impressions. Many are related to photos I've seen over and over again throughout my life. My parents would tell me stories about my childhood, and their versions of the stories would become my memories. I remember sights, sounds, smells, and feelings. The way my Aunt Amelia spoke French with a rich Peruvian accent and sang "Feliz Navidad" on the front porch at Christmas dinner; the feeling of my wet hair freezing into icicles as I walked to school on a winter day; the smell of my Grandma sautéing vegetables from her garden; the lingering smell of cigarette smoke at the amusement park.

All of these impressions paint a picture of who I am and where I came from. I won't always remember names, dates, or even places, but even that paragraph of memories above will add to my story.

What homes do you remember living in, and what did you love about each one? This may be difficult, and you may need to dig deep. Was there a certain room, corner, or wall color that you loved? Maybe you had a wonderful neighbor who made your apartment feel like home.

_____

_____

_____

_____

_____

_____

_____

_____

_____

_____

_____

What was your childhood neighborhood like? If you lived in many, list them, with a few descriptors for each.

_____

_____

_____

_____

_____

_____

_____

_____

_____

Where did you like to spend time outside your home? Did you have a favorite park or friend's house? Was there a babysitter, daycare provider, or friend who watched you while your parents were at work?

_____

_____

_____

_____

_____

_____

_____

_____

What did you contribute to your family dynamic growing up? Were you the clown? The peacemaker? The fighter? The voice of reason? The source of quiet calm?

_____

_____

_____

_____

_____

What does Christmas smell like? Thanksgiving? Easter? Your birthday? What aromas let you know it's time to celebrate?

_____

_____

_____

_____

_____

What other memories do you have from the holiday celebrations of your childhood?

_____

_____

_____

_____

_____

_____

_____

_____

_____

What was your best childhood birthday, and what made it special? Who was there? Did you receive a memorable gift?

_____

_____

_____

_____

_____

_____

_____

_____

_____

What voices stand out in your memory from childhood? Your mom's unique vibrato as she sang bedtime songs? Your grandfather's gravelly voice? The soft squeak of your kindergarten teacher?

_____

_____

_____

_____

Write about your childhood pets. Were they cuddly? Slimy? Family pets? Something you kept in a jar in the backyard? What did you gain from connecting with animals as a child? If you lived a pet-free existence, write about that.

_____
_____
_____
_____
_____
_____
_____
_____
_____

What's the first thing you can remember wanting to be when you grew up? What drew you to that profession?

_____
_____
_____
_____
_____
_____

How did that dream stretch you or make you work harder?

_____
_____
_____
_____
_____
_____

What were your hobbies as a kid? Did you play with Transformers? Nurse your dolls? Watch TV all day?

_____

_____

_____

_____

_____

_____

What interesting things did you collect as a child? What was the prize of your collection?

_____

_____

_____

_____

_____

_____

What clothes can you remember from your child-hood that made you feel special? How did you obtain them? Where did you wear them?

_____

_____

_____

_____

_____

_____

_____

_____

_____

_____

_____

What is the craziest thing you ever did as a child?

_____

_____

_____

_____

_____

_____

_____

_____

_____

When I was around seven years old, I desperately wanted to break my arm or leg. A couple of kids at school had showed up to class with a cast and become instant celebrities. The casts looked cool, and everyone gave the invalids so much attention.

So I started jumping out of trees with my arms crossed and my knees locked in hopes of injuring myself. Then at the slightest bruise, I would wail and beg my mom to take me in for X-rays.

Years later, as an adult, I sat nervously on a table waiting for an ankle X-ray. To pass time in the awkward silence, I told that story to the X-ray technician.

"Yeah," he said, "there's a name for people like that. They have an actual disorder."

I think it's called Childhood.

What pranks did you pull on your siblings or parents?

_____

_____

_____

_____

_____

_____

_____

_____

Write down some of your favorite childhood jokes.

_____

_____

_____

_____

_____

If you had to describe your childhood in one sentence, what would that sentence be?

_____

_____

_____

_____

_____

How would you describe your childhood in one word?

_____

SCHOOL YEARS

So much of who I am today has roots that extend back into my school years. The friends I made, the teachers who influenced me, the lessons I learned, and the games I played all helped to form me. The memories of your school years will likely be a little clearer than those of your early childhood, but there will still be tons of details that are hazy, and that's okay.

Whether or not you remember the name of the middle school PE teacher who finally convinced you to wear deodorant is not as important as the knowledge that you no longer smell bad. So write about that teacher. He deserves a sentence in your Bucket of Awesome even if you refer to him only as Seventh Grade PE Teacher. If you have a yearbook lying around and want to look him up later and add his name to the story, go for it.

For some people, school days were filled with wonder, magic, and friendship. Some of us had a harder time with school, due to either our unique learning styles or social skills. Some of us had great teachers and excellent schools, while others struggled to learn in environments that were less than ideal.

Please remember that the questions in this autobiographical exercise are meant to focus on the aspects of your life story that built you up, that added the Awesome to who you are today. Respect the struggles.

Feel the struggles. Then move on. Choose to write your story of triumph. Your elementary school was a black hole? Find the spark of joy at the bottom of the pit, the teacher who inspired, the friend who cared, the bus driver who smiled, or the lesson you learned when you surfaced from the trial.

Whether or not you attended a traditional school, the following questions can help you mine your memories for the best of your early learning experiences.

ELEMENTARY SCHOOL

Where did you attend elementary school?

_____

_____

_____

_____

_____

_____

What did your school look like? Smell like? Feel like?

_____

_____

_____

_____

_____

_____

_____

_____

_____

_____

What did you love most about your school?

_____

_____

_____

_____

_____

_____

In what ways do you feel you are a better person for having been educated in that place?

_____

_____

_____

_____

_____

_____

_____

_____

If you had to choose one subject to study all day, what would it have been and why?

_____

_____

_____

_____

_____

_____

_____

_____

What are some crazy fads you and your friends went through? Were there bands you loved or maybe suddenly hated when they were no longer cool? Whose face did you wish was tattooed on your bedsheets when you were in fifth grade?

_____

_____

_____

_____

_____

_____

_____

_____

_____

What was the coolest toy you ever had as a child? How did you obtain it?

_____

_____

_____

_____

_____

_____

What was your first experience with money of your own? Did it happen in your childhood years or not until much later?

_____

_____

_____

_____

_____

_____

What kind of student were you? What were your strengths?

_____

_____

_____

_____

_____

_____

What did you have to work extra hard on in school?

_____

_____

_____

_____

_____

Who was your favorite elementary school teacher? What did that teacher do and say to make you love him or her so much?

_____

_____

_____

_____

_____

What games did you play at recess?

_____

_____

_____

_____

How would you describe your elementary school social style? Were you shy or outgoing? Did you have many friends or just one or two good ones?

_____

_____

_____

_____

_____

_____

_____

_____

If you spent a lot of time alone as a child, what were some of the good things about that independence? How was your experience different from what you see children experiencing today?

_____

_____

_____

_____

_____

_____

_____

_____

_____

_____

_____

_____

_____

How did you get to school? Did you take the bus, walk, ride in a car, or ride your bike? What are your best memories from your commute to school?

_____

_____

_____

_____

_____

_____

What did you do for meals during elementary school?

_____

_____

_____

_____

_____

_____

Is there a particular food that brings you back to a place of comfort and nostalgia? What was it? What did you love about it, and who prepared it for you?

_____

_____

_____

_____

_____

_____

_____

_____

_____

_____

What are five things you're glad you learned early in life? Who taught them to you?

_____

_____

_____

_____

_____

_____

_____

_____

MIDDLE SCHOOL

A word about middle school or junior high—this can be a really rough time for a lot of people, myself included. I've struggled with the question, "Why do we even have to go through those difficult years?" The answer I've come up with is that we go through them so we can successfully tackle what comes after. Both literally and symbolically, we would not be the people we are today, ready to face the challenges of adulthood, without some hard growing experiences. And while it's awful to feel mocked, lonely, insecure, or painfully awkward, there are things about our experiences in middle school that shape us for the better. Can you join me in looking for the good?

What was the name of your middle school or junior high school? How would you describe it in one sentence or less?

_____
_____
_____
_____
_____
_____

What was positive about middle school? List anything you can think of: a teacher you liked, the excitement of getting to use a locker for the first time, band friends, track team, coming home at the end of the day and knowing someone loved you.

_____
_____
_____
_____
_____
_____
_____
_____
_____

Who loved you in middle school? How did you know it?

_____
_____
_____
_____
_____
_____

What friends or family members could you not have lived without during your tween years? Why?

_____

_____

_____

_____

_____

_____

_____

_____

How did your experiences in middle school change the course of your life for the better?

_____

_____

_____

_____

_____

_____

_____

_____

Maybe some things changed the course of your life for the worse, but we're focusing on ones that made a positive change. For me, the bullying helped me build empathy and compassion. I am kinder because I witnessed so much unkindness and even because I tried a little unkindness out for myself and hated how it felt.

In what happy ways did you stand out from other kids in your school, whether you were happy about being different at the time or not?

_____

_____

_____

_____

_____

_____

What was your coolest middle school outfit?

_____

_____

_____

_____

_____

_____

Can you remember an instance when you stood up for someone who was being bullied or gave service to another student? Can you think of a time you wish you had? What did you learn from that experience, regardless of what action you took?

_____

_____

_____

_____

_____

_____

_____

_____

_____

I remember a boy named Manuel who was the target of intense bullying on my junior high school bus. I kept my head down and tried to ignore it, afraid that if I took a stand against the bullies, I would also become a target. I'm not proud of the way I handled things, but I did learn an important lesson. It doesn't feel good to do nothing when you have the power to do something. I like to think that experience and the way I felt has made me more willing to stand up for someone who needs my help in the future.

What extracurricular activities did you participate in, and how did they affect your life?

_____

_____

_____

_____

_____

_____

_____

_____

What memorable teachers or mentors touched your life during these years? What did you learn from them?

_____

_____

_____

_____

_____

_____

What's the most difficult thing you overcame in middle school?

_____

_____

_____

_____

_____

_____

What did you get better at in the years between elementary school and high school?

_____

_____

_____

_____

_____

_____

If you could go back and visit your twelve-year-old self now, what would you tell him or her?

_____

_____

_____

_____

_____

_____

_____

_____

_____

_____

_____

HIGH SCHOOL

Did you attend traditional high school or get your
education some other way? What factors affected
your decision, and what did you hope to gain from
your experiences?

_____

_____

_____

_____

_____

_____

Where did you attend high school?

_____

If you were writing a promotional ad to get people
to come to your high school, what things would you
include? Be sincere. What are the selling features of
your high school? What did you love about it?

_____

_____

_____

_____

_____

_____

_____

_____

_____

_____

_____

_____

_____

Who was the most influential teacher you had in high school? Why did he or she make such a difference in your life? Describe him or her. What did you learn from him or her?

_____

_____

_____

_____

_____

_____

_____

_____

Did you make any sacrifices in high school? How did that experience impact you? What I'm talking about here are choices you had to make to give up something you loved for something more important. Did you drop out of band so you could focus on your calculus class? Did you need to give up social time so you could get a job and help support your family?

_____

_____

_____

_____

_____

_____

_____

_____

_____

_____

_____

What sports, clubs, or extracurricular activities were you involved in? Write about them.

_____

_____

_____

_____

_____

_____

_____

_____

_____

What activities did you enjoy outside of school as a teenager?

_____

_____

_____

_____

_____

_____

_____

_____

What was your high school learning style? Did you take advantage of your learning opportunities? Did you need external motivation?

_____

_____

_____

_____

_____

If you could relive a single day in high school, what would it be?

_____
_____
_____
_____
_____
_____
_____
_____
_____

How was your high school a better place because you were there? Even if it was just one act, one day, what did you do to improve the lives of your fellow students, teachers, or high school employees?

_____
_____
_____
_____
_____
_____
_____
_____

If your graduating class voted you most likely to do or be something, what was it or what would it have been?

_____
_____
_____
_____

Do you remember any of your school principals? What did you learn about leadership and mentoring from watching them lead?

_____

_____

_____

_____

_____

_____

_____

_____

Did you graduate from high school? Was it easy, or did you struggle? Who supported you as you worked toward your diploma?

_____

_____

_____

_____

_____

_____

_____

_____

_____

_____

_____

_____

_____

What were your big dreams and plans after high school? Did you have your life mapped out or fly by the seat of your pants? If you had a plan, did you follow through or did life take you in a different direction?

_____

_____

_____

_____

_____

_____

_____

_____

If you did not complete high school, what did you gain while you were there or what did you learn by leaving early?

_____

_____

_____

_____

_____

Who were your closest friends as a teenager? What brought you together?

_____

_____

_____

_____

_____

_____

_____

Did you ever attend a school dance or celebration? If yes, describe it. What did you wear? Who did you go with? What was it like?

_____

_____

_____

_____

_____

_____

_____

_____

What's one thing you would change about the choices you made in high school? How can you incorporate that change into your life today?

_____

_____

_____

_____

_____

_____

_____

_____

_____

_____

_____

_____

_____

_____

_____

_____

ADULTHOOD

*S*o you turn eighteen, and suddenly, you are an adult. You spend your life saying, "When I grow up . . ." and then you do, and honestly, you don't feel all that different. At first printing of this book, I'm in my thirties and I still have goals about what I'm going to do and be when I grow up. Luckily, we never really stop growing and changing.

But being an adult means all kinds of new privileges and responsibilities. You may be the same on the inside, but the way the world sees you is different and the types of experiences you can have change as well.

Let's talk about some of the Awesome that happened as you made the transition to adulthood.

(If you have not yet made the transition to adulthood, move on to the love chapter and fill this out in a few years.)

YOUNG ADULTHOOD

At what age did you consider yourself an adult? How would you define adulthood?

_____
_____
_____
_____
_____
_____

When did you first feel responsible for yourself, like you knew it was up to you to decide how your life would go?

_____

_____

_____

_____

_____

_____

What was your first home away from your parents or guardians? What do you remember about that home?

_____

_____

_____

_____

_____

_____

Describe your first night on your own.

_____

_____

_____

_____

_____

_____

Who did you live with when you moved out of your childhood home?

_____

_____

_____

_____

Now that you do your own grocery shopping, what are your favorite grown-up foods?

_____

_____

_____

_____

_____

_____

Write your craziest roommate story.

_____

_____

_____

_____

_____

_____

_____

_____

What experiences from your young life prepared you for adulthood?

_____

_____

_____

_____

_____

_____

_____

_____

_____

What character strengths helped you adjust to life on your own?

_____

_____

_____

_____

_____

When have you been involved in an issue, supported a cause, or taken action politically? Have you voted? Have you ever volunteered? Posted a sign on a lawn or a message on Facebook to call people to action? What civic actions do you care about?

_____

_____

_____

_____

_____

_____

_____

_____

_____

My sophomore year of high school in Calgary, Alberta, there was serious unrest about teacher salaries. On a certain day, a group of student activists had orchestrated a massive walkout. High school students all over the city were encouraged to get up at a specific time, exit their classes, and march downtown to city hall.

I talked to my mom about it the night before, and she asked me not to do it. I agreed.

But when the hour came and our teacher said, "I know what you're planning to do, and I won't stop you from walking out," and all my fellow classmates got up and left, I decided to leave with them. I got swept up in a mob of students chanting and singing and marching down the middle of the main highway in town.

Roads were closed. Reporters were everywhere. I was part of something big! Although, the truth was, I had no idea what I was protesting.

That night, it was more than a little mortifying to explain this to my mother who then told me that since I cared so much about the budget disputes, she would drive me downtown to watch the salary negotiations all day on a Saturday.

Since then, I've learned to be a little more informed, and when I stand up for something, I make sure I mean it.

What do you consider to be your most important educational experience in young adulthood? Did you travel? Attend college or vocational school? Receive on-the-job training?

_____

_____

_____

_____

How were your educational experiences as an adult different from your earlier learning experiences? How did they prepare you for your future career?

_____

_____

_____

_____

_____

What's a big mistake that you made while trying on adulthood, and how did you fix it? Who helped you? What did you learn that you will never forget?

_____

_____

_____

_____

_____

_____

_____

_____

OLDER ADULTHOOD

When did you first feel old? This can be mature, like as a child getting to do something big, or as an adult, feeling OLD.

_____

_____

_____

What's the best thing about aging?

_____

_____

_____

_____

_____

_____

What makes you feel young?

_____

_____

_____

_____

_____

_____

In my thirties, I developed a love of bike riding. I call my friend Stephanie and ask her to join me for a ride. There's something about picking up my friend, putting on our dorky helmets, and riding along the trail that makes me feel about ten years old. "Can Stephanie come out and play?"

In what aspects of your life and personality do you consider yourself mature?

_____

_____

_____

_____

_____

_____

How would you most like to develop your character in the next ten years?

_____

_____

_____

_____

_____

_____

_____

_____

What was your first major purchase as an adult? How did you prepare and save for it, and how did you feel when you signed the papers or made your first payment?

_____

_____

_____

_____

_____

_____

_____

_____

As an adult, who are the people you know love you?

_____

_____

_____

_____

_____

_____

Who do you love the most?

_____

_____

_____

_____

_____

_____

_____

_____

Now that you are older, what aspects of childhood
are you nostalgic for?

_____

_____

_____

_____

_____

What things do you do now that you never thought
you'd do when you were younger?

_____

_____

_____

_____

_____

_____

_____

_____

_____

_____

What are your favorite privileges of adulthood?

_____

_____

_____

_____

_____

_____

What roles and responsibilities do you fill that bring
you the most pride?

_____

_____

_____

_____

_____

What relationships have you formed that define your
adulthood? In what ways do they strengthen you?

_____

_____

_____

_____

_____

_____

_____

_____

_____

_____

_____

_____

What are your favorite holidays now? Why?

_____
_____
_____
_____
_____
_____

What special things do you do to celebrate these holidays? Do they all come from your childhood or have they developed over time?

_____
_____
_____
_____
_____
_____
_____
_____
_____

What other traditions do you keep?

_____
_____
_____
_____
_____
_____
_____
_____
_____
_____

LOVE

Experiences with love will look different to every person. Even two siblings growing up in the same home will give, receive, and perceive love differently. You may have lived a warm, cuddly existence full of hugs, snuggles, and bouquets of roses. Possibly, love is something you struggle to feel for others or recognize from them. Most people are in the middle of those two extremes. However, every person in this world has been touched in some way by love. Love is the magic. It builds. It inspires us to be our best selves. Love gives joy and color to our lives. This section will focus on finding places where you have given or received love in your life.

As you're answering these questions, please remember that comparison is the thief of joy. When writing about the dynamics of love in your life, you may think, "They loved my brother more." Okay. Maybe they did. But we're not talking about him. We're talking about you. What love did *you* feel from your parents? Find the joy in your gifts and choose not to be the victim of the world's inequality.

When was the first time you knew you were loved? How did you know you were loved? If this love happened at an age earlier than your brain can reliably remember, have you heard stories about things others did for you to show love?

_____

_____

_____

_____

_____

_____

_____

_____

_____

_____

_____

_____

_____

My dad worked his butt off in school to earn a degree that would allow him to support his family. He never liked accounting, but he did it for his wife and his kids. When I was a young child, my dad was in graduate school. He loved and cared for his kids by working hard and providing for us.

Who were the members of your immediate family growing up? What do you love most about each of them?

_____

_____

_____

_____

_____

_____

_____

_____

What is your family's love style? Are you mushy-gushy? Stoic? Tender? Silly? How do you show each other how you feel?

_____

_____

_____

_____

_____

What does the word *family* mean to you?

_____

_____

_____

_____

_____

_____

_____

_____

_____

Who is your family now? Avoid a formulaic answer here. Whether you live alone, you live with roommates, or you're married and raising twenty kids, who do you consider to be your family? How do you define that relationship?

_____
_____
_____
_____
_____
_____
_____
_____
_____

What do you love most about each member of your current family?

_____
_____
_____
_____
_____
_____
_____
_____
_____
_____
_____
_____
_____
_____
_____
_____

List the strengths of your parents' relationship. What did you learn from watching them together? If they didn't get along, what did you learn about relationships from watching them struggle?

_____

_____

_____

_____

_____

_____

_____

_____

_____

If you're a parent, when and how did you decide to have kids?

_____

_____

_____

_____

_____

How has becoming a parent changed you? How has it positively changed your relationship with your partner?

_____

_____

_____

_____

_____

_____

What are the most rewarding things about raising children?

_____

_____

_____

_____

_____

_____

If you don't have children, what's the biggest perk about not having them?

_____

_____

_____

_____

_____

If you are a parent, tell the story of how your children came into your life.

_____

_____

_____

_____

_____

_____

_____

_____

_____

_____

_____

_____

My husband and I always planned to have at least four children, but largely due to health concerns, we were certain we were done after our third was born. This was extremely painful to me. I cried whenever I thought about it for several months after we made the decision.

Then one day I looked around at my three kids and our wonderful life and I thought about all the blessings of having a smaller family than we had originally intended. Vacations are easier and less expensive. We'll be done with the business of raising young children sooner, so we can pursue other goals. Our small home is plenty big for our needs. The more I thought about it, the more I realized that although our life isn't following our ideal plan, there are perks to the path we're traveling.

What are some of your favorite memories from raising your children?

_____

_____

_____

_____

_____

_____

_____

_____

_____

_____

_____

How are your children like you? In what ways have they surprised and delighted you?

_____

_____

_____

_____

_____

_____

Write about experiences you've had loving or mentoring another person.

_____

_____

_____

_____

_____

_____

_____

_____

What was your favorite family vacation from your childhood? From adulthood?

_____

_____

_____

_____

_____

_____

_____

_____

_____

How would you describe "good times" with your family? What counts as quality time?

_____

_____

_____

_____

_____

_____

What is the biggest growing experience you've had with your family?

_____

_____

_____

_____

_____

If you have siblings, how have your relationships with them evolved over time?

_____

_____

_____

_____

_____

_____

_____

_____

_____

_____

What is your strongest image of your father? Your mother?

_____

_____

_____

_____

_____

_____

_____

_____

_____

FRIENDS

Sometimes, your family members are friends, and other times, your friends can become so close they feel like family. Let's write a little bit about the friends who have made a difference in your life.

What makes a good friend?

_____

_____

_____

_____

_____

_____

_____

_____

_____

_____

_____

Who was your first friend or the first friend you remember? How did you meet him or her? Do you remember his or her name? What did you like to do together?

_____

_____

_____

_____

_____

_____

What games did you play with friends growing up? What was a typical playdate?

_____

_____

_____

_____

_____

If you have time to spend with friends now, what do you do?

_____

_____

_____

Who knows you better than anyone? How did he or she come to know you so well?

_____

_____

_____

_____

_____

_____

What sort of physical touch do you like to give and receive from your friends? What makes you feel loved? Hugs? Kisses on the cheek? An arm around your shoulders? A three-foot, touch-free radius?

_____

_____

_____

_____

_____

_____

Can you think of a time someone cried with you?

_____

_____

_____

_____

_____

Have there been times in your life when you felt alone or lonely? What skills did you develop as you coped with that situation and those feelings?

_____

_____

_____

_____

_____

_____

_____

_____

_____

What friends have showed you the way or mentored you? How has their influence changed your life for the better?

_____

_____

_____

_____

_____

_____

_____

_____

_____

If your friends were asked to give one reason they valued your friendship, what reason would they give?

_____

_____

_____

What does goodness look like? Describe someone you know who is truly good. (This person can be living or dead.) What did they do to show their goodness? In what ways do you try to be like them?

_____

_____

_____

_____

_____

_____

_____

_____

_____

_____

What's the most memorable gift you've ever received? It's okay if there's more than one.

_____

_____

_____

_____

_____

_____

What's the coolest gift you've ever given to someone? Who was it for, and what made it so special?

_____

_____

_____

_____

_____

_____

What was the last thing that made you laugh so hard you couldn't breathe?

_____

_____

_____

_____

_____

_____

Who makes you laugh more than anyone else in your life?

_____

_____

_____

_____

_____

In my family, we have a time-honored tradition called "horkeling." To horkel means to laugh so hard at the dinner table that your beverage shoots out your nose. It was my role in the family to time my silliness perfectly to make as many people at the table horkel as possible. I'm proud to say I've gotten nearly every member of my immediate family. That takes skill.

ROMANCE

Have you ever been in love? This may be hard to define. You may have had butterflies when you were around someone, experienced a full-on romance, or loved someone from afar. It's messy. It's complicated. But loving and being attracted to someone can also be a huge source of joy. Use this section to explore how loving and possibly being loved romantically has made your life sparkle. If you have yet to experience mutual romantic love, know you are not alone. There are many people still waiting for this fulfillment and many more who have had love but lost it. Remember that you can only control the choices you make, the love you give. Loving others is the best thing you can do to bring love into your life.

What is your definition of love? Has it changed over time?

_____

_____

_____

_____

Have you ever had a crush on someone? Kissed someone for the first time? Experienced true romance? Write about your romantic firsts.

_____

_____

_____

_____

_____

_____

_____

_____

List your most influential romantic partners and what you loved about them or what good you gained from the relationships.

_____

_____

_____

_____

_____

_____

_____

_____

_____

_____

_____

_____

_____

_____

_____

If you are currently in a relationship, what is the "origin story" of that relationship? In other words, how did you meet? If you're not currently in a relationship, do you have a funny or interesting story about the start of a past relationship?

_____

_____

_____

_____

_____

_____

_____

_____

_____

If you are married or in a long-term committed relationship, how or when did you know your partner was "the one?"

_____

_____

_____

_____

_____

_____

Were you and your love in love from the start, or did building the relationship take time?

_____

_____

_____

_____

_____

_____

Describe what it is like to know someone is truly smitten with you. How does your life change when you know someone can't live without you? If you've never experienced this, write about what you imagine this will feel like in the future.

_____

_____

_____

_____

_____

_____

_____

_____

What happens to you when you feel intense romantic love? How are you improved by those feelings?

_____

_____

_____

_____

_____

When I am in love, I try harder. I try harder to look my best, to be kind, to ignore the faults of my true love. When I am in love, my cheeks glow, my eyes sparkle, and I truly look better. I feel better. My confidence grows, and my faith in humanity increases. When I am in love, I feel an increased sense of hope and possibility.

Have you ever loved someone and those feelings were not returned? Oh, mama. I have. When I think about it, I still feel pain in my gut. What did your unrequited love teach you about what you want in a partner and what you needed to change about yourself or your expectations?

_____

_____

_____

_____

_____

_____

_____

_____

Have you ever worked hard on a relationship? What were the good fruits of that labor, even if it didn't work out in the end?

_____

_____

_____

_____

_____

_____

_____

_____

_____

_____

_____

_____

Were you ever separated from someone you loved? How did being apart strengthen you either as a person or in your relationship?

_____

_____

_____

_____

_____

_____

In your opinion, why do we need romantic relationships? What's the point?

_____

_____

_____

_____

_____

_____

What is the greatest thing you offer as a romantic partner?

_____

_____

_____

_____

_____

_____

_____

_____

_____

_____

_____

_____

What is your relationship advice? What makes a strong marriage or relationship?

_____
_____
_____
_____
_____
_____
_____
_____
_____
_____
_____
_____
_____
_____
_____
_____
_____
_____
_____
_____
_____
_____
_____
_____
_____
_____

WORK

Sometimes, we get paid in money for the work we do. I like those times. Other times, we just work because stuff needs to get done. Nearly any time we work, we learn something, even if it's just that our lives are better when we work hard—even if we don't always enjoy it.

Who was your greatest example of work, and how did he or she teach you?

_____

_____

_____

_____

_____

_____

_____

_____

_____

When in your life did you work the hardest?

_____

_____

_____

_____

_____

_____

_____

_____

Write about any odd jobs or money-making ventures
you participated in as a child or teen.

_____

_____

_____

_____

_____

_____

What was your first job?

_____

_____

_____

_____

_____

Write about the first time you were paid for working
at a "real job." Was it as much as you expected? How
did it feel to hold that money in your hands or see it
materialize in your bank account? What did you do
with it?

_____

_____

_____

_____

_____

_____

_____

_____

_____

What jobs have you held?

_____

_____

_____

_____

_____

_____

_____

_____

_____

Make a list of your marketable skills. What can you
do that people are willing to pay you money for?
What skills do you have that people aren't willing to
pay you nearly enough for? (You might not necessarily want to do these things for a living.)

_____

_____

_____

_____

_____

_____

_____

*People frequently ask me if I will sell them the
hats I crochet for my kids. At the rate I crochet,
they'd have to pay me $60 per hat to make it
worth my time, but I still consider crocheting
one of my marketable skills. People would pay
to see these moves.*

What motivates you to work hard?

_____

_____

_____

_____

_____

_____

What was your favorite job? Why did you love it so much?

_____

_____

_____

_____

_____

_____

Name one job you are grateful to be done with. Even though you didn't enjoy it, what did you learn?

_____

_____

_____

_____

_____

_____

Did your career have any major turning points? Write about them.

_____

_____

_____

_____

_____

_____

Have you ever changed careers? What gave you the courage to make the switch, and what was the result?

_____

_____

_____

_____

_____

_____

If changing careers is a dream of yours, what would that transition look like—and what's holding you back?

_____

_____

_____

_____

_____

What bosses or work supervisors have influenced you or mentored you professionally? What did they do to have such an impact on your life?

_____

_____

_____

_____

_____

_____

_____

_____

_____

_____

How would you define yourself professionally? What do you "do"?

_____

_____

_____

_____

_____

_____

What small things do you do on the job that make you stand out?

_____

_____

_____

_____

_____

_____

What formal education have you had in your life? List the schools or training programs you attended. What degrees or certifications have you earned, and how have they helped you in your career?

_____

_____

_____

_____

_____

_____

_____

_____

_____

What informal education prepared you to make a living?

_____

_____

_____

_____

_____

_____

_____

_____

_____

_____

_____

_____

_____

_____

_____

_____

_____

_____

_____

_____

_____

_____

_____

_____

_____

RESILIENCE AND STRUGGLES

My kids can look at a perfectly lovely pizza and say, "Ewwww! Mushrooms!" They don't see the bread or the sauce or the cheese. They only see mushrooms. The worst pizza ever. But if I pick off the two or three offending pieces of fungi, they are able to notice the deliciousness of everything else that's sitting there on their plates.

This is the reason we've been trying to focus so much on what's good in our lives. We've been pulling the mushrooms to the side so we could see the amazing pizza of our lives. I mean, what's the good in having these massively amazing lives if all we see are the mushrooms?

So, we've been pretty Pollyanna with this writing adventure so far. *What do you love about your life? What are you Awesome at? Share your greatest experiences!* But not all experiences feel great at the time, and frequently, the experiences that make us great are not all that fun. Here's where we talk about those. It's time to call attention to the hard times. Not in a whining, complaining, or victimized way, but in a way that empowers us to choose whether we will be crushed by our suffering or rise up strong.

You can't choose your past. You *can* choose what you keep, what you focus on, how you tell your story, and how you write the next chapter.

Is it the low before the high? Were you building a comeback? Some of the best, most inspiring stories, even comedies, begin with tragedy, heartache, or simple stagnation. They were going nowhere UNTIL THEY WENT SOMEWHERE!

We can do hard things.

We can write about hard things.

We can learn from hard things.

HARD TIMES

What were the most difficult times of your life?

_____
_____
_____
_____
_____
_____

What made them so hard?

_____
_____
_____
_____
_____
_____
_____
_____
_____

How did you get through them?

_____

_____

_____

_____

_____

_____

_____

_____

_____

In college, I directed a documentary about rape and sexual assault. I was interviewing counselors, law enforcement professionals, and survivors. For months, my life was consumed with stories of brutal violence and injustice. And, to top it off, my team was coming apart at the seams. There was fighting between the crew members and ultimatums from faculty that I needed to fire members of my team who had been as much a part of conceptualizing the film as I had.

I was called horrible names and felt like I was being torn in half. I started developing a stomach ulcer and experienced panic attacks for the first time in my adult life. It was brutal.

But out of that experience came a film I'm proud of, something that's been shown to countless women to encourage them to get the help they need after an assault. I learned where to turn for strength in hard times, and I learned some really painful lessons about how to interact with and treat people in charged situations.

There was some truth to the names I was called. I was immature and inexperienced as a leader. And I made some pretty epic and hurtful mistakes.

I would never want to go through that again. However, when I look back on that year, I am incredibly grateful for the personal growth I experienced.

Were there any people who helped you make it through or guided you to learn from what you experienced? Who were they, and what did they do to help you?

_____

_____

_____

_____

_____

_____

How are you stronger today because of your trials?

_____

_____

_____

_____

_____

_____

_____

_____

What other lessons in your life have you learned the hard way?

_____

_____

_____

_____

_____

_____

When everything goes wrong, who is your first phone call? Why?

_____

_____

_____

_____

_____

_____

Write about a time your tough experience allowed you to mentor someone else through a trial.

_____

_____

_____

_____

_____

_____

_____

_____

_____

_____

_____

List the character traits you possess that you wouldn't be blessed with if your life had always been smooth and perfect.

_____

_____

_____

_____

_____

_____

Do you have any strong memories of weather events? Were there storms, heavy snowfall, or other natural phenomena that marked certain periods of your life? Tell about the weather of your life, possibly coinciding with different seasons of your life or different places you've lived.

_____

_____

_____

_____

_____

_____

What major world events or conflicts had a significant impact on your life? Take as much time as you need to explain what you lived through and how it shaped you for the better.

_____

_____

_____

_____

_____

_____

I was working at a public library when the second plane hit the World Trade Center on September 11th, 2001. One of the librarians came and told everyone what had happened, and the floor dropped out from under me.

I was young, fresh out of college, living alone as a full-fledged adult for the first time, hundreds of miles from my family. And suddenly, one thing was clear. I needed to be with Dan.

We had only been dating for about a month, but when the world seemed on the brink of destruction, he was the one I ran to. The thought came flooding to my mind: I wish we were married. If everything else in my life were ripped away, there would be comfort in knowing we would be together.

We were married four months later. There were many factors involved in our lightning-fast courtship, but the uncertainty of everything after 9/11 really helped move us along. Fill your grocery cart with bread, and batteries, and bottled water. Focus on what matters. Be with the people you love. You never know what will happen tomorrow.

A DIFFICULT PAST

A word about jerks and abusers—we let jerks win when we accept what they give us, carry it around, and build our lives around it. If I get an ugly sweater for Christmas, either by some well-meaning person who doesn't realize how horrible it is or by someone hell-bent on making sure she always looks better than me, I can keep it, toss it, or simply keep the cute earrings that came with it. I choose whether I welcome it into my life and build my wardrobe around it. I don't need to regift it, sharing my negative experience with others. I don't need to accuse every other gift-giver in the future of giving me an ugly sweater before I even open up the wrapping paper.

Don't let someone else's choice dictate your future. Don't pass your hurt and anger on to other people. Don't let one terrible person taint your view of all the new wonderful people you meet. There really are more good people in the world than bad. Don't let the exceptions color your world with negativity.

What have you learned through being mistreated by another person? How are you stronger now because of your experiences?

_____

_____

_____

_____

_____

_____

_____

_____

_____

_____

_____

_____

_____

_____

What ways have you found to help other people without being consumed by their problems?

_____

_____

_____

_____

_____

_____

Have you ever struggled with physical or mental illness or injury? Write about it. What did you gain from that experience?

_____

_____

_____

_____

_____

_____

_____

_____

_____

_____

_____

_____

_____

_____

_____

_____

_____

_____

Write about a time when you lost something that really mattered to you. A contest? An election? A prized possession? A relationship? What did you gain by losing? You may have to stretch as you think about this. Maybe you gained greater understanding or an increased desire to try.

_____

_____

_____

_____

_____

_____

_____

_____

_____

_____

_____

_____

_____

In sixth grade, I ran for class president. I made cupcakes, signs, and flyers. I wooed the public. And I lost. I couldn't believe it. How could anyone not vote for me?! For the first time in my life, I didn't achieve what I set out to do.

This was a great low-stakes way for me to realize that you don't always get what you want but you have to keep trying, and after a night of crying, life always goes on. This is comforting to me as I litter agents' inboxes with my fiction manuscripts.

What is the best worst thing to ever happen to you, something that helped you grow in unexpected ways?

_____

_____

_____

_____

_____

_____

_____

_____

Write about a time you failed and tried again.

_____

_____

_____

_____

_____

_____

_____

Can you think of any happy accidents in your life, things that didn't necessarily go right but ended up Awesome?

_____

_____

_____

_____

_____

Who is your favorite example of perseverance? Why?

_____

_____

_____

_____

_____

_____

What would you tell your current or future child to
help him or her get through a harrowing experience?

_____

_____

_____

_____

_____

_____

_____

_____

_____

_____

_____

_____

_____

_____

_____

_____

_____

_____

_____

CHARACTER

Your thoughts, choices, and experiences stack on each other one by one to build your story and character. If you fail and keep trying, you're building resilience and persistence. If you manage to tell the truth one time when it would be a whole lot easier to lie, you're developing honesty. In this section, we'll talk about the experiences that have shaped your core values and character.

FAITH

Let's talk about faith.

As you're answering these questions, be thoughtful about your true feelings and most intimate beliefs. What actually gives purpose and meaning to your life? Not "What do you think is supposed to give purpose and meaning to your life?"

What do you believe in? What is the force or power that fuels you to go on, that gives purpose to your life?

_____

_____

_____

_____

_____

_____

_____

In what faith tradition, if any, were you raised? How did you benefit from what you were taught?

_____

_____

_____

_____

_____

_____

What was beautiful about the faith of your childhood?

_____

_____

_____

_____

_____

_____

○ *Often, people who have left their family faith and find a new path suddenly decide that everything about their religious upbringing was repressive and horrible. They lose the ability to see any good.*

I had a similar experience with New Kids on the Block *in sixth grade. I loved them. They were the best. I couldn't get enough of their slick hair, rockin' dance moves, and squeaky voices. But when they went down in flames and were suddenly the definition of LOSERLY in the realm of sixth-grade popularity, I destroyed their cassette tapes and burned all of their posters in my backyard barbecue pit. Oh,*

Jordan Knight, what did you ever do to me? Where I once thought they were super hot and fabulous, I suddenly couldn't believe I had liked anyone so totally annoying.

But there was good to NKOTB. They were my first band crush, one of my first experiences with boy-induced butterflies. I had many giggling dance parties with my friends to their music. They taught me to hang tough. So many good memories.

I'm not saying your childhood religious traditions are like a boy band. What I am saying is that you will be happier if you focus on the good and what you've gained from your past. Don't discount everything, even if you've decided to put your past behind you.

What experiences have led you to find peace with your spiritual path as an adult?

_____

_____

_____

_____

_____

_____

_____

_____

_____

_____

_____

_____

How does your adult spirituality differ from your childlike belief?

_____

_____

_____

_____

_____

_____

What do you do to feel peace?

_____

_____

_____

_____

_____

For years, NPR ran a segment called "This I Believe," in which people read essays expressing their core beliefs. The range of these essays covered everything from spiritual truth to the Beatles, and it became clear that while we are all different, we all have strong beliefs and opinions that inform the way we see and interact with the world. What is one truth you know for sure?

_____

_____

_____

_____

_____

_____

_____

What positive character traits have you developed because of your beliefs?

_____

_____

_____

_____

_____

_____

What message about your beliefs would you like to pass on to the next generation?

_____

_____

_____

_____

_____

_____

_____

RELATIONSHIPS

What three words best describe the way you participate in relationships?

_____

_____

_____

_____

_____

Write about a time when a stranger was kind to you. Have you ever had a need that was filled by someone who didn't even know you?

_____

_____

_____

_____

_____

_____

I was driving in downtown Seattle after exiting a busy conference, and the streets were jammed with people heading for the freeways. Unfamiliar with this part of town, I watched for the freeway signs and found myself desperately trying to get over just one more lane so I could enter I-5. The woman in the lane to my right refused to let me in. I gestured to her. She shook her head. Frustrated, I inched toward her lane, made eye contact, and mouthed "Please." She rolled down her window to speak with me.

"Don't you realize that both of these lanes merge onto the freeway?" she said kindly. "In fact, the lane you're in is a better lane for merging."

I did not know it. And I was grateful to her for showing me the way.

When have you acted as the kind stranger? What prompted you to jump in and help?

_____

_____

_____

_____

_____

_____

Did you ever walk by and not help someone in need? What did you learn from that experience?

_____

_____

_____

_____

_____

_____

Write about a time you were forgiven. Did you deserve to be forgiven? What effect did that mercy have on you?

_____

_____

_____

_____

_____

_____

_____

_____

_____

_____

_____

What are your greatest strengths in relationships? As a friend? As a family member?

_____

_____

_____

_____

_____

_____

_____

_____

What makes a good parent, and how do you try to incorporate those traits into your life? How did you learn this definition?

_____

_____

_____

_____

_____

_____

_____

_____

_____

_____

_____

_____

_____

_____

_____

_____

PERSONAL

Can you remember a time you cried for joy? Is this a frequent occurrence? What makes you cry happy tears?

_____

_____

_____

_____

_____

_____

_____

_____

_____

List five things you love about yourself, and write stories that exhibit how you've shown those attributes.

_____

_____

_____

_____

_____

_____

_____

_____

_____

_____

_____

_____

_____

_____

_____

What talents have you shown a spark for or spent time developing? How have those skills and abilities blessed your life and the lives of others?

_____

_____

_____

_____

_____

_____

_____

_____

_____

I took art in high school all the way through until twelfth grade. I wasn't the most amazing artist, but I enjoyed creating. As my senior year drew to a close, my art teacher took me aside and told me I didn't need to complete the final project, a portfolio of my work.

"You're not going to use art in the future anyways, so I don't want you to waste the time."

Ouch.

I put away my art supplies that day, and it was nearly twenty years before I had the guts to try sketching again. I had spent years of my life developing my love and talent for art, and I let one person destroy that. Hopefully, as you make a list of talents you have been passionate about throughout your life, you will rekindle some old flames and pursue some endeavors that make you happy.

How do you create? If you want to generate something beautiful or interesting, what do you do? What are your favorite creative outlets?

_____

_____

_____

_____

_____

_____

_____

_____

Have sports or other physical activities played a major role in your life? What do you love to do with your body? What effect has this had on your life?

_____

_____

_____

_____

_____

_____

_____

_____

_____

_____

_____

_____

_____

_____

What were your favorite books as a child? As a teenager? As an adult? Right now? Elaborate on why you love them.

_____

_____

_____

_____

_____

_____

_____

_____

_____

_____

_____

_____

What is your favorite part of the day? Why? Has it always been your favorite? If not, what made the difference for you?

_____

_____

_____

_____

_____

_____

_____

_____

_____

_____

_____

_____

A cheerful friend once told me that she hadn't always been a morning person. In fact, she'd always hated mornings. But then one day she decided she was sick of being miserable when she woke up.

She decided to start pretending she loved mornings.

She would put on a fake smile and greet people warmly. After a few months of this, she was surprised to realize she really did love mornings.

If you could design your own heaven, what would it be like?

_____
_____
_____
_____
_____
_____

How can you incorporate aspects of that reality into your daily life now?

_____
_____
_____
_____
_____
_____
_____
_____
_____
_____

What are you a fan of? Who or what would you hang posters of on your wall or cheer for out loud?

_____

_____

_____

_____

_____

_____

What are you grateful for in January? List each month and think of all the things you look forward to when it comes around.

_____

_____

_____

_____

_____

_____

_____

_____

_____

_____

_____

_____

_____

_____

_____

_____

_____

_____

_____

_____

January is the start of a new year. March means spring is almost here. June is Flag Day in the United States, and there's nothing more exciting than studying flag lore!

If you were to break your life up into seasons, what would they be? What did you enjoy most about each season?

_____

_____

_____

_____

_____

_____

_____

_____

_____

What is your current season in life? What do you hope the next one involves?

_____

_____

_____

_____

_____

If you could develop any personal strength that you currently lack, what would it be?

_____

_____

_____

_____

_____

What are your big goals?

_____
_____
_____
_____
_____
_____

Can you think of a time when you were on top of
the world, when you thought you could accomplish
anything?

_____
_____
_____
_____
_____
_____

What ingredients went into building that feeling?

_____
_____
_____
_____
_____
_____

What are you the absolute best at?

_____
_____
_____
_____
_____
_____

Who believes in you the most? Why?

_____

_____

_____

_____

_____

_____

_____

_____

_____

_____

_____

_____

_____

_____

_____

_____

_____

_____

_____

_____

_____

_____

_____

_____

_____

_____

_____

_____

_____

_____

ACCOMPLISHMENTS

Imagine it's your funeral, and someone stands up to give your eulogy. This is the big show, the chance for someone to list all the great things you've ever accomplished. It's like the ultimate post-game analysis. What did Kathryn accomplish? Why did her life matter? The nice thing about a eulogy is, if it's done correctly, it doesn't read like a résumé, because the speaker drills down to the accomplishments that really matter. Sure, if you won an Oscar, it would probably get some airtime, but I imagine more focus would go to how kind you were to your children or your accomplishments serving in your community.

Sometimes it's hard to think of our own accomplishments. "Well, I didn't really do all that much," we say. Sometimes it's false modesty, but often we really can't see all the good we do. I want you to think hard about what you've done that matters. What have you accomplished in your life?

You need to dig deep and be honest with yourself as you're answering these questions. There may be times when you don't feel great about yourself, when you can't imagine why anyone else is glad you're around, but I want you to step outside yourself for just a moment and try to think about why you're loved, why people want you in their lives.

WHO YOU ARE

Create a quick bullet list of things that should be
included in your eulogy.

_____

_____

_____

_____

_____

_____

_____

_____

_____

_____

_____

_____

What is on your bucket list? Include items you've
already checked off that were must-dos in your
lifetime.

_____

_____

_____

_____

_____

_____

_____

_____

_____

_____

_____

_____

Whose life have you saved? Even a little? Have you saved someone from starving, from drowning, from ending his or her life? Have you made decisions that have affected the health or living conditions of another person? Were you ever a conscientious driver? Did you ever rescue someone who was alone, disoriented, or afraid? Write about it.

_____

_____

_____

_____

_____

_____

What is the best advice you've ever received, and how has it helped your life?

_____

_____

_____

_____

_____

What are the turning points of your life?

_____

_____

_____

_____

_____

_____

_____

_____

Write about a time you said "No" and it was a good thing.

_____

_____

_____

_____

_____

_____

Write about a time when you said "Yes" and it was good, even if it was hard.

_____

_____

_____

_____

_____

_____

What was one time when you felt beautiful (or handsome), inside or out? Why did you feel that way, and how did it feel?

_____

_____

_____

_____

_____

_____

Given all the things you've learned in your life, what are three things you absolutely know?

_____

_____

_____

_____

What would you tell your twenty-year-old self to help him or her be happier now? Write it to yourself now.

_____

_____

_____

_____

_____

_____

_____

_____

_____

How are you better today than you were ten years ago?

_____

_____

_____

_____

_____

_____

_____

_____

What would you consider to be your greatest accomplishment, and why?

_____

_____

_____

_____

_____

_____

_____

_____

Channeling Jimmy Stewart in *It's a Wonderful Life*, how is the world different, in Awesome ways, because you are part of it?

_____

_____

_____

_____

_____

_____

Did you have a hard time on that last one? Think of this—is there a person you know who is glad you are alive? Who is it, and why?

_____

_____

_____

_____

_____

_____

FEATS

What feats of strength or stamina have you surprised yourself by completing?

_____

_____

_____

_____

_____

_____

Can you think of a time you didn't think you could go on but you managed to stay strong? Describe how you convinced yourself to keep going and how it felt when you finished.

_____

_____

_____

_____

_____

_____

_____

_____

In my early thirties, giving in to positive peer pressure, I started signing up to complete athletic events with my friends. They were marathon runners, and I was the girl who had never run a mile without stopping. I started out slow, drafting off their patience and kindness, and I sort of stayed there.

To this day, I have never placed in a race. In fact, I'm still happy simply to finish, but I complete what I start and I push myself harder each time.

During the final leg of my second triathlon, I was struggling. I couldn't run anymore. I had no strength left. But I told myself that even if I couldn't run anymore, I could walk in the shape of a run. I slowed down to a walk but kept my body in a running position. It was possibly the slowest "run" ever recorded, but I knew that if I kept going, I would feel triumphant for finishing the race strong. And I did it!

People with visual impairment often report improved hearing. Because of their weakness in one area, their abilities are strengthened in another. What weaknesses do you possess that have helped you to grow? How have they become strengths?

_____

_____

_____

_____

_____

_____

Sometimes our greatest feats of strength are accomplished in our relationships with other people. Have you ever been kind to someone who was hard to love? With or without naming names, write about the experience.

_____

_____

_____

_____

_____

_____

_____

_____

_____

_____

_____

Write about a relationship that tested or increased
your strength.

_____
_____
_____
_____
_____
_____
_____
_____
_____
_____
_____
_____
_____
_____
_____
_____
_____
_____
_____
_____
_____
_____
_____
_____
_____
_____
_____

ALL THE REST

As you've worked through this book, I've guided you through all kinds of questions that spring from my life experience or the experiences of my friends and readers. However, the most beautiful thing about life is that no two people are exactly the same.

So here's your chance to use your uniqueness to write about the things I haven't asked you about. What more do you need to say? What stories need to be told?

Never stop telling your story, and always be conscious of how you tell it. Ask yourself, "What stories can I tell that will be the most helpful and productive in my future life? What backstory do I want my future superhero self to have?"

Write that.

Focus on that.

I wish you love and joy as you continue to write and tell your story. Your life will be beautiful. Choose to see it for what it truly is.

_____

_____

_____

_____

_____

_____

I'VE HEARD THEM SAY

I'm sure you realize that you're not the only person who has stories to tell about your life. Your family, friends, neighbors, and coworkers could add richness and depth to your biography. If you feel comfortable, ask some of your closest friends and family to share memories about you.

Modify one of the prompts from the book, or simply ask them to write about how you met, describe their most important memory of you, or write a paragraph describing you.

Turn this section into the back page of your high school yearbook, but forbid anyone from writing "Keep in touch" or "Have a great summer."

_____

_____

_____

_____

_____

_____

_____

_____

_____

_____

_____

_____

_____

_____

_____

_____

_____

ABOUT YOU—AGAIN

You're not dead yet. Your story goes on, and you will continue to evolve and grow over time. As things change, keep adding to your Bucket of Awesome. One way to keep the journey going is to fill out the About Me section again every five years and watch how your tastes and opinions change over time. Here are a few pages to get you through the next twenty years.

_____

_____

_____

_____

_____

_____

_____

_____

_____

_____

_____

_____

_____

_____

_____

_____

_____

_____

_____

_____

_____

_____

_____

ABOUT ME

Today's date: _____

Name: _____

Date of birth: _____

Place of birth: _____

Names and birthdates of parents and grandparents:

_____

_____

_____

_____

Names of people in your home as you grew up:

_____

_____

_____

_____

Education: _____

Vocation: _____

Eye color: _____

Hair color: _____

Favorite food: _____

Favorite color: _____

Hobbies: _____

Greatest accomplishment: _____

Thing you're most likely to spend discretionary funds on: _____

Favorite books, magazines, websites, or other reading material: _____

Favorite movies or TV shows: _____

What location do you consider to be "home"?

_____

ABOUT ME

Today's date: _____

Name: _____

Date of birth: _____

Place of birth: _____

Names and birthdates of parents and grandparents:

_____

_____

_____

_____

Names of people in your home as you grew up:

_____

_____

_____

_____

Education: _____

Vocation: _____

Eye color: _____

Hair color: _____

Favorite food: _____

Favorite color: _____

Hobbies: _____

Greatest accomplishment: _____

Thing you're most likely to spend discretionary funds on: _____

Favorite books, magazines, websites, or other reading material: _____

Favorite movies or TV shows: _____

What location do you consider to be "home"?

_____

ABOUT ME

Today's date: _____

Name: _____

Date of birth: _____

Place of birth: _____

Names and birthdates of parents and grandparents:

_____

_____

_____

_____

Names of people in your home as you grew up:

_____

_____

_____

_____

Education: _____

Vocation: _____

Eye color: _____

Hair color: _____

Favorite food: _____

Favorite color: _____

Hobbies: _____

Greatest accomplishment: _____

Thing you're most likely to spend discretionary funds on: _____

Favorite books, magazines, websites, or other reading material: _____

Favorite movies or TV shows: _____

What location do you consider to be "home"?

_____

ABOUT ME

Today's date: _____

Name: _____

Date of birth: _____

Place of birth: _____

Names and birthdates of parents and grandparents:

_____

_____

_____

_____

Names of people in your home as you grew up:

_____

_____

_____

_____

Education: _____

Vocation: _____

Eye color: _____

Hair color: _____

Favorite food: _____

Favorite color: _____

Hobbies: _____

Greatest accomplishment: _____

Thing you're most likely to spend discretionary funds on: _____

Favorite books, magazines, websites, or other reading material: _____

Favorite movies or TV shows: _____

What location do you consider to be "home"?

_____

ACKNOWLEDGMENTS

I want to give a shoutout to KayLynn, Dan, and Heather for helping shape this project.

Thank you to my friends, family, and readers for sharing your amazing stories with me. And thank you to everyone at Familius for helping make the world a better place.